I0821583

CLASSIC ROCK BANDS

PINK FLOYD

by Todd Kortemeier

CONTENT CONSULTANT
Shaugn O'Donnell
Music Department Chair
The City College of New York

An Imprint of Abdo Publishing | abdobooks.com

abdobooks.com

Published by Abdo Publishing, a division of ABDO, PO Box 398166, Minneapolis, Minnesota 55439.

Printed in the United States of America, North Mankato, Minnesota.
052021
092021

Cover Photo: Michael Ochs Archives/Getty Images
Interior Photos: Globe Photos/MediaPunch/IPX/AP Images, 4–5; Lefteris Pitarakis/AP Images, 9, 12–13; Michael Ochs Archives/Getty Images, 14–15, 36–37; Andrew Whittuck/Redferns/Getty Images, 19, 26–27; Adam Ritchie/Redferns/Getty Images, 22–23, 29; AP Images, 34, 76–77; Chris Walter/WireImage/Getty Images, 41; Romain Fellens/picture-alliance/dpa/AP Images, 44; PA Wire URN:6351399/Press Association/AP Images, 46–47; Hans D'rrwald/picture-alliance/dpa/AP Images, 49, 62; Ian Francis/Shutterstock Images, 54; Steve Morley/Redferns/Getty Images, 56–57; Marco Saracco/Shutterstock Images, 64; Gijsbert Hanekroot/Alamy, 66–67; DWD-Media/Alamy, 70; Bob Child/AP Images, 75; Andreas Schoelzel/AP Images, 80–81; Hansjoerg Krauss/AP Images, 84; Joseph Sohm/Shutterstock Images, 88–89; Fabio Diena/Shutterstock Images, 92, 95

Editor: Melissa York
Series Designer: Colleen McLaren

Library of Congress Control Number: 2019954389

Publisher's Cataloging-in-Publication Data

Names: Kortemeier, Todd, author.
Title: Pink Floyd / by Todd Kortemeier
Description: Minneapolis, Minnesota : Abdo Publishing, 2022 | Series: Classic rock bands | Includes online resources and index.
Identifiers: ISBN 9781532192012 (lib. bdg.) | ISBN 9781532179914 (ebook)
Subjects: LCSH: Pink Floyd (Musical group)--Juvenile literature. | Rock and roll bands--Biography--Juvenile literature. | Rock musicians--England--Biography--Juvenile literature. | Psychedelic rock music--Juvenile literature. | Progressive rock music--Juvenile literature.
Classification: DDC 782.42166--dc23

CONTENTS

CHAPTER ONE

Back in London

Night had fallen on Hyde Park in London, England, on July 2, 2005. Approximately 200,000 people were gathered to witness history.[1] A lot of them couldn't even see the stage. They had to watch on screens placed throughout the park.

As the lights went down, the familiar sound of a heartbeat played over the speakers. It was the intro to one of Pink Floyd's greatest albums, 1973's *The Dark Side of the Moon*. The album used a lot of sound effects, something Pink Floyd was famous for. *Dark Side* was one of the first concept albums, with all the songs focused around central themes.

From left to right, Pink Floyd's David Gilmour, Roger Waters, Nick Mason, and Richard Wright

Hyde Park

Hyde Park has been an important concert venue since the late 1960s. In fact, Pink Floyd performed in the first-ever concert in the park on June 29, 1968. The concert was free and included fellow rockers T. Rex and Jethro Tull. Some of the world's biggest musicians have played Hyde Park in the decades since, from rock band the Rolling Stones to pop star Taylor Swift.

The band soared through the opening track off the album. David Gilmour's vocals were as solid as ever. Roger Waters couldn't help but sing along to himself as he ripped through his bass part. Nick Mason kept a steady time on the drums. Richard Wright's keyboards added to and filled out the sound. A screen behind the quartet showed visuals of the moon and famous symbols from the band's career. Pink Floyd was also famous for the visual component of their shows.

On the band's journey to stardom, it lost founding member Syd Barrett, replacing him following his excessive drug use and erratic behavior. Barrett's absence always haunted the band, even as it became bigger and more successful. By the late 1970s, personal conflicts doomed Pink Floyd. Waters, another founding member, left in 1985, and the band was never the same. But Pink Floyd's journey brought them back to London 20 years later to perform at musician

Bob Geldof's Live 8 charity concert.

Geldof wanted the biggest names in music there to raise as much money as possible, so he called up Waters. Waters was interested, but he knew Gilmour would have to be convinced. Waters was so out of touch with Gilmour that he didn't even have his old friend's phone number. He had to get it from Geldof. It was the cause that convinced the guitarist. Doing a reunion for charity was the one way to get Gilmour to the stage. Mason and Wright were already on board.

Live Aid

Live 8 in 2005 was a tribute to the legendary Live Aid concert of 1985. Both were organized by Bob Geldof, who in the 1980s was best known as the lead singer of the Boomtown Rats. Live Aid was a benefit concert to raise money for starving people in Africa. It lasted for 16 hours at venues around the world. More than one billion people tuned in to watch, and more than $125 million was raised (approximately $300 million in today's dollars).[2] Some of the performers included U2, Queen, and a reunited Led Zeppelin. Gilmour performed, but he was there as part of another band.

Live 8 was not only a tribute to Live Aid but also its own charity campaign. It was scheduled around the G8 summit, a meeting of eight powerful world leaders. That was also where the concert got its name. The goal of Live 8 was to encourage these leaders to boost monetary aid to and reduce the debt of poor countries.

BACK TOGETHER AGAIN

The announcement sent shock waves around the music world. The event was already drawing some huge acts. U2, Paul McCartney, Elton John, and more were scheduled to appear. A reunited Pink Floyd, together for the first time in decades, was the biggest news of all.

But what would they play? And most importantly, how would they sound? How does a band pick up where it left off after so many years? "It's sort of assumed that we'll all remember how [the songs] go," Mason said.[3]

Fortunately for all, they remembered. But picking the set list brought up old conflicts. Gilmour and Waters disagreed on which songs to play. And once they agreed on the songs, they disagreed on the arrangements they would play. Waters said later he didn't mind rolling over and not having it his way. For the most part, the band members got along well as they put together their set list. They didn't have much time to fill. Their set was only 20 minutes.

TAKING THE STAGE

The band's next song was "Money." One of Pink Floyd's top singles, it opened with sound effects of coins clinking and cash registers opening, and it featured a driving bass line by Waters. Dick Parry,

Waters' appearance at Pink Floyd's reunion amazed and delighted fans across the globe.

one of the band's longtime collaborators, came out for a saxophone solo. Gilmour expertly tore through the song's guitar solo.

The next song, "Wish You Were Here," was a special one for the band. Perhaps sensing the moment, Waters addressed the crowd for the first time. "It's actually rather emotional standing up here with these three guys after all these years," Waters said as the song's intro began.[4]

He also remembered the song's message, and how it related to their friend no longer playing beside them. "We're doing this for everyone who's not here," Waters continued, "but particularly of course for Syd."[5] Wright nodded his head in agreement. Unlike on the recording, in which Waters sang the whole song, Gilmour and Waters traded off singing the verses. While Waters sang, Gilmour at one point looked back at Mason. The two shared a smile. The band was having fun. Gilmour and Waters then sang the chorus together.

> "[David] did send me an email afterward . . . It said, 'Hi, Rog, I'm glad you made that phone call. It was fun, wasn't it?' So he obviously had fun."[7]
>
> – *Roger Waters, interview with* Rolling Stone *magazine, August 11, 2005*

To close, the band played a live favorite. It was "Comfortably Numb" off *The Wall. The Wall* was another concept album. It is considered one of the band's greatest works. The song closed with an extended guitar solo by Gilmour. It was a six-minute song on the album, but the solo stretched it out to nearly ten minutes. As it was the band's last song, nobody in the crowd seemed to mind.

A BITTERSWEET ENDING

As Gilmour strummed the last note, a sign above the stage read "NO MORE EXCUSES."[6] It referred to the indifference by world leaders to poverty.

But it also could apply to the band. There seemed to be no more excuses for not performing together.

As the crowd continued cheering, Gilmour thanked the crowd and then went to leave the stage. But Waters called him back, and the band stood arm in arm to take a bow. The reunion was complete. The band members had been able to put aside their differences and give fans one more memorable performance.

In the weeks and months that followed, fans hoped for more. There was a lot of interest in Pink Floyd working together again. The band was even offered more than $150 million to stage a tour.[8] But they turned it down.

In a way, it was a fitting legacy for the performers. Pink Floyd had produced some of the greatest music in rock history, but the group's career peak was fairly short. They made three of the greatest rock albums ever in the 1970s, and many listeners were left wanting more.

Renewed Interest

The Live 8 reunion generated a lot of interest in Pink Floyd. The band received offers to tour, and its music began to sell very well. Sales of the Pink Floyd discography increased 1,300 percent.[9] But because Live 8 was a charity concert, the band chose not to profit from the renewed interest. The money generated from record sales was donated to charity.

Gilmour thrilled fans at Live 8 with an extended version of one of his most famous guitar solos.

Fortunately, fans had plenty of great songs and memories to hold on to.

Pink Floyd recorded its first single on January 29, 1967, at a sound studio just a few miles south of Hyde Park. That song, "Arnold Layne," went to

Number 20 on the UK music charts and launched the band's career. Over the next 15 years, the quartet of college friends went on a journey together, making Number 1 records and changing rock music forever.

CHAPTER TWO

Friends and Bandmates

Some common themes ran through Pink Floyd's music even in the band's early days. Isolation, anti-war, and anti-authority themes that the band would explore years later on *The Wall* were part of the lives of two of Pink Floyd's driving forces: George Roger Waters, who went by Roger, and Roger "Syd" Barrett, who went by Syd.

Roger was born in Surrey in southeastern England on September 6, 1943, in the middle of World War II (1939–1945). Roger's father, Eric, was a teacher who did not believe in war. He claimed conscientious objector status when the war began

Mason, Wright, Barrett, and Waters, *from left to right*, formed Pink Floyd's original lineup.

and stayed out of the fighting, instead driving an ambulance.

But during the war, Eric changed his mind and enlisted as a soldier. Roger's mother, Mary, a schoolteacher, moved Roger and his brother John to Cambridge, approximately 50 miles (80 km) north of London. She thought it would be safer to be farther from the capital during the war. On February 18, 1944, Eric was killed during the Battle of Anzio in Italy. Roger was only five months old when his father died.

> "I hated every second of [school], apart from games. The regime at school was a very oppressive one."[1]
>
> – *Roger Waters, quoted in* Comfortably Numb: The Inside Story of Pink Floyd, *2008*

Though Roger never knew his father, the loss affected him greatly. He felt isolated from other boys in school who grew up having their fathers around. Roger was a good student but railed against the rigid English educational system. He believed students deserved better treatment and better teachers. The one aspect of school he enjoyed was sports, and he was a talented cricket and rugby player.

A FRIENDSHIP BEGINS

Syd Barrett was born on January 6, 1946, in Cambridge. Despite being more than two years apart, Roger and Syd knew each other. Mary Waters taught Barrett in school and the two boys became acquainted. Syd was also friends with David Gilmour, who was closer in age to him.

Syd was very artistic and enjoyed painting, writing, and making music. He was charming, but he also possessed a temper that could be violent. Syd lost his father to cancer when he was 16. The death had a profound effect on him, and he became even more dedicated to his art.

Cambridge

Most of Pink Floyd's members spent at least part of their lives in Cambridge. The town is the home of the University of Cambridge, one of the oldest educational institutions in the world. As such, Cambridge has long been known more for education than for rock music. But Pink Floyd helped change that. The town remains extremely proud of its association with the band. Fans can take tours seeing the members' childhood homes, spots where the band hung out together, and more.

Roger chose to channel his own artistic ambitions into architecture, enrolling at Regent Street Polytechnic College in London in 1962. Syd stayed in Cambridge, enrolling at the Cambridge Technical College as an art student. Seeking to bolster his

Richard Wright could play wind instruments, but keyboards were his main responsibility in Pink Floyd.

drawing skills, Roger spent time with Syd when he would return home to Cambridge.

Roger grew disillusioned with his studies and became more interested in music than architecture. He bought a guitar and started jamming with friends and playing at parties in college. He soon met two fellow students who also enjoyed music: Nick Mason and Richard Wright.

NICK AND RICHARD

Nicholas Mason was born on January 27, 1944, in Birmingham in central England. His family moved to North London when he was two. Nick played piano and violin as a child, but he didn't really take to music until he got his first drum kit at age 12. He remained devoted to the instrument, even keeping a kit in his room at Regent Street Polytechnic.

Richard Wright, born on July 28, 1943, in northwestern London, was also a musician as a youngster. Richard was a piano and trumpet player, and he taught himself to play guitar at age 12. Richard became deeply interested in jazz music after he heard an album by Miles Davis, and he decided to learn trombone and saxophone as well.

Nick, Richard, and Roger were all architecture students at Regent Street. None of them were very passionate about architecture. But they did all share a passion for music, and in the early 1960s their

tastes leaned toward jazz. The rise to prominence of bands like the Rolling Stones and the Beatles inspired more of an interest in rock and roll. The Rolling Stones were of particular influence to Roger and Syd. They once attended a show together in London featuring the Stones as the headline act. The two spent the train ride home sketching out ideas for what their band's live show would look like.

THE BAND TAKES SHAPE

Roger, Nick, Richard, and three friends of theirs formed a band called Sigma 6 at school in 1963. The band made several lineup and name changes, later becoming the Abdabs, then the Screaming Abdabs, and finally the Tea Set. Their repertoire was primarily R&B covers from the United States. Even back in those early days, bandmates recalled that Roger was very particular about what he wanted. And he

Bob Klose

Bob Klose was not an official member of Pink Floyd for long, leaving the band in 1965. But by leaving the band, he played a key role in the development of its future signature sound. Klose was more of a blues guitarist, and his departure led the band to experiment with different genres of music. Klose later became a photographer, but he never gave up music entirely. He even performed on two of Gilmour's solo records.

could be aggressive with those demands.

Pink Floyd really began to take shape once Syd moved to London in 1964. He moved into an apartment with Roger and Bob Klose, who had since joined the Tea Set. Bob was a guitarist, so Roger switched to bass. Syd became the band's lead singer and songwriter.

A problem arose when the band turned up for a gig only to discover another act called the Tea Set on the bill. Syd rifled through his record collection and combined the names of two American blues musicians, Pink Anderson and Floyd Council, to become the Pink Floyd Blues Band.

In 1965, Bob quit the band to focus on his studies. This left Roger, Nick, Richard, and Syd

Pink and Floyd

It is unknown whether the namesakes for Pink Floyd ever knew about the band they inspired. Pink Anderson and Floyd Council each died in the mid-1970s. Anderson, from South Carolina, and Council, from North Carolina, were obscure blues musicians at the time Syd Barrett discovered them. Although their songs appeared together on various early blues compilations, they likely never met one another.

"Each [concert] was a complete buzz because we did totally new things and none of us knew how the others would react to it."[2]

– *Richard Wright, interview with Nicholas Schaffner*

Psychedelic light shows were an important part of early Pink Floyd concerts.

to continue as a quartet. They also shortened the name to the Pink Floyd Sound.

BECOMING PINK FLOYD

The band was still playing its R&B tunes, but it was beginning to experiment and draw out the

compositions. The musicians played around with different sounds and sound effects, such as using a metal lighter against the guitar strings as a slide. A lot of these innovations came from Barrett. His contributions to the band were less about playing an instrument and more about experimentation and songwriting. He dreamed up new sounds and ways of creating them to enhance Pink Floyd's innovative songs.

The band also incorporated visuals into its shows. Film clips and colored lights served as a stage backdrop as they played. This experimentation earned them a following in London's underground music scene. Some of these fans enjoyed taking hallucinogenic drugs such as LSD. These drugs produced effects that enhanced visuals like the ones the Pink Floyd Sound used in their shows. The drugs were widely available within the underground music scene, and Barrett became a frequent user.

The Pink Floyd Sound remained relatively unknown but was very popular among fans of experimental music. One of these fans, Peter Jenner, was so enthusiastic about them he convinced a wealthy friend, Andrew King,

LSD

LSD, short for lysergic acid diethylamide, is a psychedelic drug. It changes the perceptions of the user so that he or she may hallucinate and experience mood changes. LSD was first developed for use in medicine and was legal. But studies soon showed potentially dangerous side effects and it was banned by the late 1960s. Psychedelic drugs were so prevalent among fans of certain kinds of music in the 1960s that a whole genre called psychedelic rock emerged around it.

to manage the band with him. Though Jenner and King knew almost nothing about the music business, they started representing the band and getting it more gigs.

CHAPTER THREE

At the Gates of Dawn

Mason went on vacation to the United States in 1966, intending to see some of the country's architecture as part of his studies. He didn't think much about the band while he was away. In fact, he thought he would rededicate himself to architecture once he returned to England. But while he was in New York City, Mason read a newspaper report about up-and-coming bands from the United Kingdom. And right there in black and white was the Pink Floyd Sound. He realized that maybe the band had more potential than he thought.

The band members reconvened later in 1966 with their new manager. Jenner was

By late 1966, the band was growing more popular, but Barrett's remaining time in the group was running out.

still learning how to manage a band, but he was able to get them a recurring gig at All Saints Hall in London. Barrett remained the driving lyrical force of the Pink Floyd Sound, writing material that went further and further away from their R&B roots.

Gaining in popularity, the band secured a gig at a benefit concert for more than 2,000 people in October 1966.[1] Though the show was in a converted railway shed and the band performed on a trailer, the group made a distinct impression on the audience. Those seeing the group for the first time were particularly awed by the light show. Jenner and King rigged up a film projector to show slides that were covered in oil, ink, and other chemicals. Once projected, these materials made beautiful and mysterious shapes as a backdrop to the performance.

By the time of the benefit concert, the band had made one final name change. Jenner had always disliked the "Sound" at the end of the name. The band dropped it and continued simply as Pink Floyd.

MAKING A RECORD

Pink Floyd became a regular performer at London's UFO Club, a haven for underground music. With its growing success, the band formed a partnership with Jenner and King called Blackhill Enterprises.

A photographer captured Pink Floyd's performance setup at the UFO Club from behind Wright's seat at the keyboard.

All six members—the band plus Jenner and King—held a one-sixth share, meaning they were equal partners in the band's success.

Pink Floyd began to think about making a record to take their music to a wider audience. UFO Club manager Joe Boyd and the band's booking agent, Bryan Morrison, agreed to fund a recording

"Arnold Layne"

Part of the reason "Arnold Layne" only reached Number 20 on the United Kingdom charts was because of its subject matter. The song is about a man who steals women's clothing off washing lines and enjoys wearing it. Even though the song does not encourage the behavior, the lyrics were very controversial at the time. The song was even banned by some radio stations.

session in January 1967. The band recorded two songs: "Arnold Layne" and "Candy and a Currant Bun." "Arnold Layne" was a fixture of their live set. The band felt it had the best potential to sell as a single.

The band got a contract offer from the record label Polydor. But Jenner and King thought they could do better and took the songs to EMI, the biggest record label in England. EMI did make a better offer and signed the band.

But "Arnold Layne" did not do as well as expected, peaking at Number 20 on the UK singles charts. A follow-up single, "See Emily Play," did much better at Number 6. That got the band a spot performing on *Top of the Pops*, a British music television show. These songs were more pop-oriented than Pink Floyd's experimental music. Long songs and strange visuals were not yet a fit for television. But Pink Floyd was growing their audience.

THE PIPER AT THE GATES OF DAWN

Pink Floyd did a lot of recording throughout the summer of 1967, and the result was their first full-length album. *The Piper at the Gates of Dawn* was released in August. It received positive reviews upon its August release, and it went to Number 6 on the UK album chart.

The EMI contract gave the band access to the best equipment and the most experienced producers. But in some cases, the band had to tone down its experimentation for its recordings. Some Pink Floyd songs stretched out to 20 minutes in a live setting.[2] The band members were also known to use all sorts of different instruments and sounds. The band learned how to use studio technology to enhance its sound. But some of the band's music was just too much for the equipment to handle. Recording the track "Interstellar Overdrive" destroyed four very expensive microphones due to the high volume.

"See Emily Play"

"See Emily Play" was Pink Floyd's second single and the first one to reach the top ten on the charts in the United Kingdom. It was also their last one for quite a while. Pink Floyd did not have another top-ten hit in the United Kingdom until 1979. The song was one of the last Barrett wrote for the band.

Next Door to Greatness

Pink Floyd was on the same record label as the Beatles, who were already international superstars when Pink Floyd joined EMI. The two bands were neighbors at Abbey Road Studios, and Paul McCartney, George Harrison, and Ringo Starr even popped in to listen as Pink Floyd recorded *The Piper at the Gates of Dawn*. McCartney was already a Pink Floyd fan. He had attended several of their shows, including their first big gig at the 1966 benefit concert.

"Syd was a changed person. He didn't appear to recognize me at first. . . . As Roger so eloquently put it later, his eyes were black holes in the sky."[3]

– David Gilmour, quoted in Pink Floyd: Behind the Wall, *2013*

THE SYD PROBLEM

The band was making hits, appearing on television, and playing to increasingly large audiences. But the band members couldn't ignore that there was a serious problem with Barrett. His behavior was getting more erratic, and it was affecting everyone.

It was no secret Barrett was a heavy drug user. But friends and bandmates, including Waters, suspected that Barrett suffered from some kind of mental health condition. Whatever the reason, Barrett had changed, and it disturbed his friends and bandmates.

Sometimes Barrett simply wouldn't turn up for gigs. Other times, he would show up but be unable to perform. In one case, Waters and Mason had to hang a guitar around his neck and walk him to the stage. But once on stage, Barrett only stood there, arms at his sides, the guitar hanging loosely. This behavior forced the band to cancel several concerts.

The band members tried to get their friend help. Waters contacted Barrett's brother, but he was unconcerned. Barrett saw doctors, but he would return in the same condition. He still had some good days, leading everyone to hope he would pull out of it. But nothing seemed to change for long.

Barrett the Writer

One of the big reasons Pink Floyd was so patient with Barrett was that he wrote almost all the band's music. On *The Piper at the Gates of Dawn*, Barrett was the lone composer listed on eight of the album's 11 tracks. He was a cowriter on two others. Waters was the only other person who had a solo composition on the album.

UNRAVELING ON TOUR

To promote *Piper*, the band embarked on its first American tour in October. It was mostly a disaster. The venues were too large and didn't suit the Pink Floyd light show. And Barrett's behavior was getting worse. He was feeling the pressure of being a recording artist while also struggling with his own mental health. At a show in Los Angeles, he rubbed a strange goo into his hair that then melted under

The high spirits of early 1967 gave way to dramatic shifts for Pink Floyd in the ensuing months and years.

the stage lights and ran down his face throughout the concert. He also detuned his guitar but played along anyway. For one TV appearance, Barrett performed properly during rehearsals but just stood there when it was time to record.

Pink Floyd finished their West Coast dates but then canceled an East Coast leg and flew home. A United Kingdom tour followed, in which the band appeared on the bill with guitar legend Jimi Hendrix and rock band the Nice. Nice guitarist Davy O'List occasionally filled in for Barrett on nights when he couldn't perform. The band began to think about a permanent replacement unless something changed in a hurry.

CHAPTER FOUR

Moving On and Changing Sides

When considering who might be a good fit to join Pink Floyd, the first name in the minds of Waters, Mason, and Wright was David Gilmour. Gilmour was known to the band, as he also came from Cambridge, though he had never been in a band with any of the members of Pink Floyd.

Gilmour was born in the Cambridge suburb of Newnham on March 6, 1946. His father was a Cambridge professor and his mother was a television producer. They encouraged their children to listen to music, and Gilmour became an early fan of rock and roll. One of the first records he bought was "Rock Around the Clock" by Bill Haley

The new lineup of Pink Floyd, including David Gilmour, *rear center*, posed for a fanciful photo session in Los Angeles in 1968.

in 1954. He was also a big fan of Elvis Presley, especially the song "Heartbreak Hotel."

Gilmour attended a different school than Barrett and Waters, but it was situated on the same Cambridge road, and the boys became acquainted. Like Barrett and Waters, Gilmour had an absent father, though his was still alive. When Gilmour was 15, his father took a job as a professor in the United States. Gilmour could have joined the family, but he chose to stay in Cambridge and moved in with family friends while trying to become a musician.

Barrett and Gilmour reconnected at Cambridge Technical College. They played guitar together often, sometimes joined by Bob Klose. But they never played in a band together until December 1967.

GILMOUR JOINS

The rest of the band members decided they had to do something about Barrett. Their first thought was to take the same approach as the American band the Beach Boys. When Beach Boys member Brian Wilson went through difficulties similar to Barret's, the band allowed him to participate as he was able. Pink Floyd did not want to go on without Barrett entirely.

Barrett agreed to this arrangement. It was Mason who asked Gilmour to join the band as a fifth member. Gilmour agreed, as his previous band, Joker's Wild, had broken up. In Pink Floyd he saw an opportunity to join a band with a record deal and a growing following.

But a five-piece Pink Floyd did not last long. Rehearsals were awkward, as Gilmour was playing and singing Barrett's parts while Barrett was standing nearby. The band played a few gigs together, but it wasn't working.

By January 1968, Pink Floyd gave up on trying to fix the problem. On the way to a gig in Southampton, someone asked Gilmour, Waters, Mason, and Wright whether they were going to pick up Barrett. The band agreed not to bother.

"Have You Got It Yet?"

One of the last songs Barrett proposed to the band was called "Have You Got It Yet?" Barrett brought the song to a rehearsal during Pink Floyd's brief run as a five-piece band. Every time the band played it, Barrett would change the arrangement so the band couldn't follow or learn it. The other members soon realized that they would never "get it" and that the whole exercise was to frustrate them. Barrett's prank on the band was likely an expression of the frustration he was feeling at the time.

AND THEN THERE WERE FOUR

Jenner and King were upset when they learned the band was simply not bringing Barrett to shows.

Barrett's departure from the band changed the direction of Pink Floyd.

While they did not deny that Gilmour was a superior guitarist to Barrett, they felt Barrett was the creative brain of the group. Nobody had told Barrett, either. He was shocked by his bandmates' decision and felt blindsided. This split the band in two, with the remaining members on one side and Jenner, King, and Barrett on the other. The band hired booking agent Bryan Morrison to manage the new quartet.

> "Roger was the one who had the courage to drive Syd out. Because he realized that as long as Syd was in the band, they couldn't keep it together."[1]
>
> *– David Gilmour, quoted in* Pink Floyd: Behind the Wall, *2013*

Despite the seemingly cold way Pink Floyd separated from their friend, it was not easy for the other members. Still, they knew they could not continue as a band with Barrett. The transition was far from seamless. Barrett seemed to not understand he was no longer in the group. Sometimes he would show up at Pink Floyd gigs and stare at Gilmour from offstage.

A SAUCERFUL OF SECRETS

Not having to deal with Barrett was a relief. But the band needed new material. They continued to perform Barrett's songs, but they also wanted to start developing a sound of their own. They had some material Barrett had worked on, but otherwise

they were starting over. Each band member made contributions, but Waters was becoming the main songwriter on the new Pink Floyd album.

That album became *A Saucerful of Secrets*. It contained the last Barrett song released by Pink Floyd, "Jugband Blues." It also contained the song "A Saucerful of Secrets," a three-part instrumental that took up most of the album's second half.

"Secrets" used many different instruments, time signatures, and sound effects to create something unlike anything the band had done before. The song is an early example of how the band used its own visual system to write music. The band did not read or write music using standard notation. Instead, they designed their own system, which Gilmour said looked like an architectural diagram. That was perhaps natural coming from his former architectural-student bandmates. The band members felt "A Saucerful of Secrets" was the best thing they had ever recorded.

> "[Our way of working was] finding something we can do individually that other people haven't tried, like provoking the most extraordinary sounds from a piano by scratching around inside it."[2]
>
> *– Nick Mason, quoted in* Pink Floyd: Behind the Wall, *2013*

The album's cover was designed by Storm Thorgerson

and his Hipgnosis collective of artists. Thorgerson was also from Cambridge and knew the band members from school. This was the first Pink Floyd artwork designed by Hipgnosis, and it was the start of a long-running association. The type of artwork Hipgnosis created was an excellent match for the band's style—surreal, mysterious, and sometimes humorous.

Hipgnosis

Some of the world's most famous album covers indirectly owe their existence to Pink Floyd. Pink Floyd asked Storm Thorgerson to design the album cover for *A Saucerful of Secrets* because the members knew him as an art student from Cambridge. Because of Pink Floyd's association with EMI, Thorgerson then got more design work and founded a studio called Hipgnosis with Aubrey Powell. Hipgnosis went on to create many of the most iconic Pink Floyd album covers as well as covers for rock bands including Led Zeppelin, Genesis, and many more.

A Saucerful of Secrets was released on June 29, 1968, the same day Pink Floyd played the first free concert in Hyde Park. It was not as successful as the band's debut album, but it did spawn a second US tour where it played some festivals.

MORE AND *UMMAGUMMA*

Waters gradually emerged as the new creative voice in the band. Experimentation remained a priority so the group members could develop the sound they were all looking for. After working

The surreal *Ummagumma* album cover showed the band next to a nested series of images of itself, each with the members in different positions.

More

Pink Floyd worked on a pair of film soundtracks in the late 1960s. First was a little-known independent film called *The Committee* in 1968. *More* was a romantic drama released in 1969. The band's music was heard not only as background in the film but also as the music whenever the radio or television was heard on-screen. Gilmour, Wright, and Mason composed the music, and Waters wrote the lyrics.

on the soundtrack for the film *More* in 1969, the band went on to release its next album, *Ummagumma*.

Ummagumma featured a unique creative process. The first half of the album was a live recording of some of the band's greatest hits to that point. The second side featured a composition from each band member.

While the record was received positively, the band considered it a failed experiment. They realized that the music was better if they worked together instead of independently. *Ummagumma* hit Number 5 on the UK album chart, becoming the band's most successful release to date.

Getting Barrett Back to Work

Barrett was out of Pink Floyd but not out of music entirely. His manager urged him to pursue a solo career, and Barrett recorded seven tracks in May and June of 1968. The songs were never finished because Barrett was difficult to work with. In 1969, Gilmour and Waters were recruited to try to work with Barrett in the studio. The result was 1970's *The Madcap Laughs*, which only hit Number 40 on the UK album chart.

CHAPTER FIVE

The Dam Breaks Open

Pink Floyd's next album started with a simple chord sequence. Gilmour played it during a rehearsal, and when Waters heard it, he thought it sounded like a score for a film. Waters wanted to flesh it out with brass instruments and a choir.

Waters hired composer Ron Geesin to finish out the track. The song became the title track off *Atom Heart Mother*, and at 25 minutes, it took up the whole first side. The second side was once again dedicated to experimentation. One of the most notable tracks was "Alan's Psychedelic Breakfast." This track included the sounds of band crew member Alan Stile preparing breakfast.

The members of Pink Floyd board an airplane for a tour in the early 1970s. This decade would see the band reach its peak of success.

In the years after Barrett's departure, Waters began taking on more responsibility for shaping the band's direction.

Hipgnosis designed the album cover. But unlike Pink Floyd's previous colorful and psychedelic covers, the cover of *Atom Heart Mother* was plain. It was a photograph of a dairy cow standing in a field. The band asked for something ordinary and unlike what they'd done before. A friend suggested to Storm Thorgerson there was nothing more ordinary than a cow. Thorgerson drove out to the countryside and photographed the first one he saw.

Atom Heart Mother rose to Number 1 on the UK album charts. It was the first time Pink Floyd had topped the charts. The band toured for most of 1970. Sometimes an orchestra joined the live shows, giving audience members a unique experience.

MEDDLING

The next Pink Floyd album started with a single note played on the piano. The band ran it through a speaker that made the sound appear to move, like the sound of a passing car. This sound developed into the song "Echoes," which was the marquee track off 1971's *Meddle*.

"Echoes" was again a long composition that was a whole side of the record, lasting more than 23 minutes. It was at times slow and meandering, using quiet moments to give the music a sense of atmosphere. Combined with Gilmour's excellent

SUNSET

> "But I think we all thought—and Roger definitely thought—that a lot of the lyrics that we had been using were a little too indirect. There was definitely a feeling that the words were going to be very clear and specific. That was a big leap forward."[1]
>
> *– David Gilmour, on the change in the band's lyrics by 1971, in an interview with* Rolling Stone *magazine, 2003*

guitar work, the band members felt "Echoes" showed a lot of progress, and they were proud of it. Waters was especially proud of his lyrics that focused on empathy, something that would become a common theme of his work.

Meddle did not do as well as *Atom Heart Mother* but still made it to Number 3 on the UK album charts. Nonetheless, the band was excited about the album and toured it extensively. They were on the road when ideas for their next album began to take shape.

TURNING ON THE DARK

Pink Floyd started talking about their next album in December 1971. With a full touring schedule already outlined, they planned to use the tour as an opportunity to keep editing and arranging material they'd already written. Waters suggested they use the album to explore a set of related themes. It would be about life and all the pressures and problems that people face.

The band made a list of these problems, things as small as the stress of travel and as big as the fear of dying. Waters would write all the lyrics. All four band members contributed at least some music.

The new album would eventually be named *The Dark Side of the Moon*. It was recorded in pieces throughout 1972. In addition to touring, the band recorded a soundtrack called *Obscured by Clouds* for the French film *La Vallee*. Pink Floyd also filmed a documentary in which they played live in the ruins of the ancient Roman city of Pompeii in Italy. The film was an artistic statement, featuring the band playing for no audience and instead showcasing the performance.

The new album's theme gave the band more direction. They wrote songs with the album's concept in mind rather than creating independent works. The band began to

The Dark Side of Oz

A phenomenon surrounding *The Dark Side of the Moon* began to emerge in the years following the album's release. Fans noticed that some of the moments on the album coincide with moments in the 1939 film *The Wizard of Oz*. By starting the album at exactly the right moment in the film, the two works seem to sync up. For example, when Gilmour sings "Look around" in the song "Breathe," the film character Dorothy turns her head around. Later, the song "Money" starts just as the film makes its iconic switch from black and white to color. The band has denied any intentional references to the film, but it remains a bit of fun and speculation for fans.

play some of the new songs on the road, and they were well received, including by music journalists. The album got its title as it was going through the final recording stages.

Sound effects again played a big role. The effects all tied in with the album's theme and added to the statement the band was making. "Money" featured the sound of cash registers ringing up sales and coins clinking together. On "Time" there were antique clocks chiming all at once. And there was a heartbeat at the beginning of the album's opener, "Breathe." *Dark Side* was about the course of a person's life from birth to death.

Clare Torry

Clare Torry didn't know what she was getting into when she turned up at Abbey Road Studios in January 1973. She was hired to sing vocals, but no words, for a Pink Floyd song, and that was all she knew. The band gave her total freedom to improvise. She heard the music and came up with some vocals she hoped fit, but she left the studio thinking they probably would not be satisfied.

However, her vocals were used in "The Great Gig in the Sky" on *Dark Side*. Torry didn't even know the band used her vocals until she picked up a copy of the album. She was paid 30 pounds (approximately $400 in 2020 dollars) for her work, but she later sued EMI and Pink Floyd for a writing credit on the song.[2] She won and earned compensation for her place in rock history.

BACK TO NUMBER 1

The Dark Side of the Moon was released in March 1973. The band was very happy with the cover, which was again designed by Hipgnosis. It featured a prism fracturing light into a rainbow that spilled across a black background. Of several proposed designs, the band chose this one immediately. It went on to become one of the most famous album covers in rock history.

The album sold well, including in the United States, becoming Pink Floyd's first US Number 1 record. It only spent one week at the top, but it had remarkable staying power, remaining on the US charts for the next 15 years.[3] The only reason

The Famous Prism

Richard Wright told Hipgnosis that the band wanted something simple for *The Dark Side of the Moon*'s album cover. Thorgerson recalled a picture of a prism he had seen in a physics textbook. The light breaking up into a rainbow reminded him of the lights used in Pink Floyd's live shows. Hipgnosis turned the prism and rainbow image from the cover upside down for the back of the album. This gave the effect of light splitting into a rainbow on the front and then meshing back together on the back. The inside of the album visually depicted a heartbeat, with blips in a line like what is seen on a heart monitor. This connected to the album's theme of life and death. The album sleeve also held stickers and a poster of pyramid shapes for fans to study and interpret as they wished.

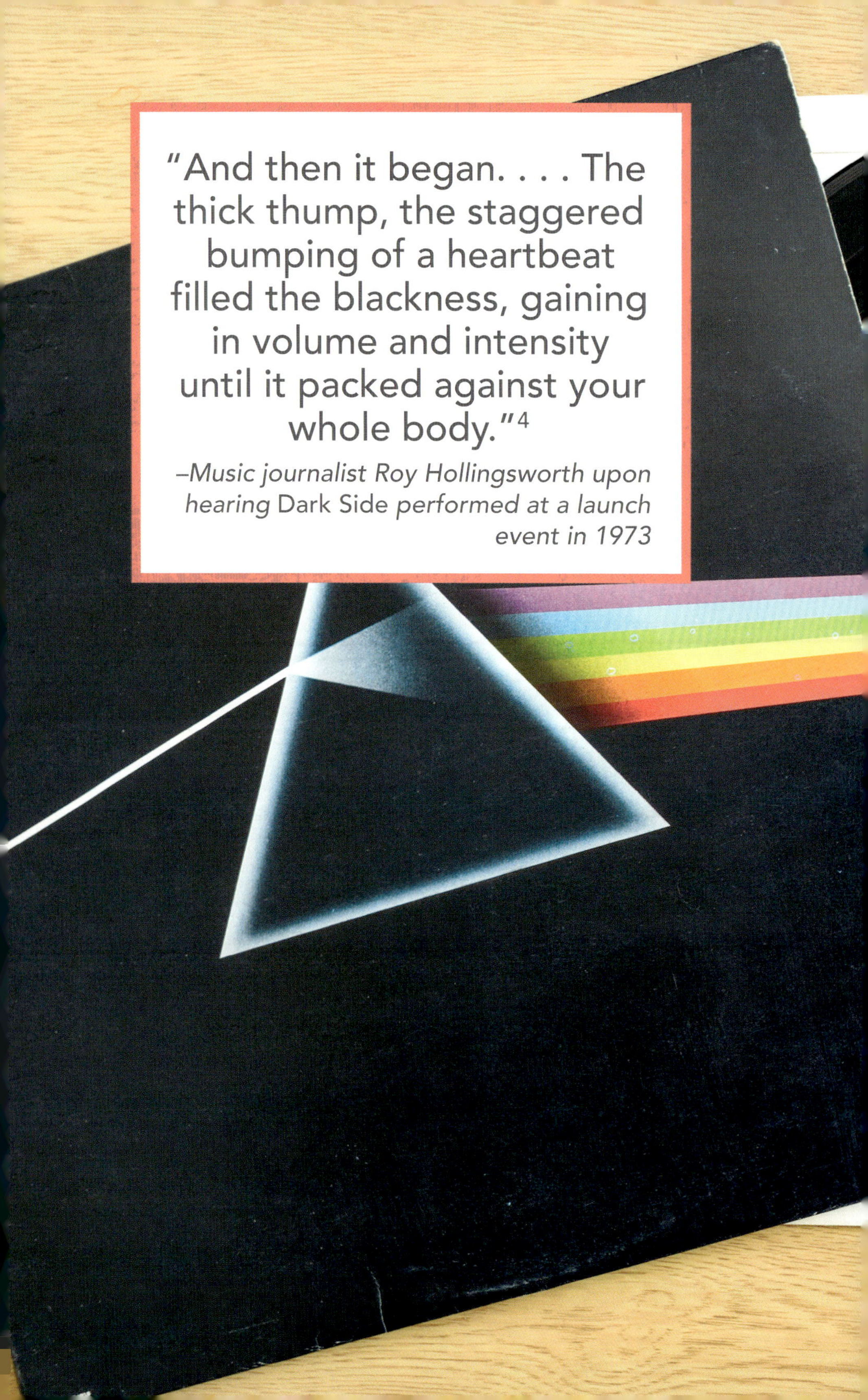

"And then it began. . . . The thick thump, the staggered bumping of a heartbeat filled the blackness, gaining in volume and intensity until it packed against your whole body."[4]

–Music journalist Roy Hollingsworth upon hearing Dark Side *performed at a launch event in 1973*

The Dark Side of the Moon became the band's most popular, enduring, and influential work.

it dropped off was because of a change in how albums were classified.

Dark Side's release was timed exceptionally well. Higher-quality stereos were becoming available to the public, and the intricate sounds of the album took advantage of that technology. The instrumentals and sound effects came through with crystal clarity. Pink Floyd was incredibly happy with the record and believed it would do well. But they didn't expect it to become one of the defining albums of the era. *Dark Side* changed their lives and set off an incredible run of success for Pink Floyd throughout the 1970s.

"On the Run"

Pink Floyd used the latest technology to record *The Dark Side of the Moon*. One example of this was the song "On the Run." The track contains no sung vocals and was created with an electronic instrument called a synthesizer. The synthesizer played an eight-note sequence sped up to create a reverberating sound. Sound effects, such as the sound of footsteps, were also added on top. As the music switches back and forth between speakers, it sounds like the footsteps are running side to side.

CHAPTER SIX

The Same Old Fears

Pink Floyd discovered the pressure of success when it came to recording a follow-up to *The Dark Side of the Moon*. The band felt that it had to match or outdo the success of that album. But they also were concerned about merely imitating what had worked about *Dark Side*.

They did not need to produce any new material right away. The band tinkered with a project called "Household Objects" in 1973. They recorded samples of normal everyday sounds, such as spraying aerosol cans, and laid them out so that they could be played like a keyboard. Ultimately

Dark Side brought the band to new heights, but the band members also felt the stress of trying to match their own iconic work.

nothing came from this experimentation, and the band took some time off.

Some band members were busy raising families and working on side projects while the band continued to tour sporadically. But as they struggled to produce new music, the shows were not up to their standards, and tensions were high. Mason felt the band was close to splitting up, at least temporarily. But by January 1975, the bandmates were back in the studio to produce a new album.

Mason's Cars

Once Pink Floyd found success in the early 1970s, Mason had the money to spend on his biggest passion besides music: collecting and racing cars. Mason's father was an amateur race car driver, and Mason grew up loving cars as well. He continued the hobby throughout his life and eventually owned many rare cars, including a racing version of a 1996 McLaren F1 that was the first of its kind made legal for the street.

A FRESH START

Pink Floyd felt that three of the songs they tested on the road would work on a new album. Only one ended up on the record. At first called "Shine On," it later evolved into "Shine On You Crazy Diamond." It opened the album that would be titled *Wish You Were Here*.

Wish You Were Here is often interpreted as a tribute to Syd Barrett, and it was in part. But Waters was also writing the lyrics to himself and the band. Now facing the pressures of success, they felt disconnected from each other as friends. They were more like workers on a project just trying to get it right. The album was about that loss of friendship as well as the loss of Barrett.

Waters composed two more songs, "Welcome to the Machine" and "Have a Cigar," that both criticized the record industry. The songs echoed the band's frustrations as they tried to make something creative while facing the pressure to make money. In all, it was a difficult period for Pink Floyd but one that ultimately produced another iconic album.

Which One's Pink?

Pink Floyd's unusual name confused some people, even record executives. They were used to people asking them whether Pink was the name of a person in the band. The song "Have a Cigar" off *Wish You Were Here* references this confusion. The song imagines a record executive speaking to the band. All he cares about is how much money the band can make for the label and doesn't know anything about them. He even asks, "Oh by the way, which one's Pink?"[1]

A VISIT FROM A FRIEND

Perhaps the most difficult part of the *Wish You Were Here* recording sessions came on June 5, 1975. Mason walked into the studio control room to see a large bald man he didn't recognize. Thinking it was a friend of one of the engineers, he carried on.

It was Gilmour who told him it was Barrett. The band members had not seen him for years, and his physical appearance had changed dramatically. But there he was, in the studio, while his former bandmates were recording music about him.

The band members had some conversations with Barrett, but they struggled to make sense of his words. He was quiet, withdrawn, and not as they remembered him back when he was fronting Pink Floyd. The whole experience was deeply upsetting. It filled the band with guilt over how Barrett was asked to leave Pink Floyd, and it further drove home the sadness of the songs they were working on. Waters was so upset that he was left in tears. As strangely as he appeared, Barrett was soon gone. The band went back to work.

BUILDING AND REBUILDING

Wish You Were Here was released in September 1975. It went right to the top of the charts in both the United States and United Kingdom. Pink Floyd had been playing several of the songs live for months in advance of its release, but there was no tour following the album's debut. The band was far from idle, though. They bought a three-story building in London and started making their own recording studio. Abbey Road was a fine studio, but Pink Floyd was continuing to expand their sound and needed something special.

Called Britannia Row, the new studio was completed in early 1976. The first project the band worked on there was a new album. Two of the songs originally intended for *Wish You Were Here* were the basis of the new work. They were called "Raving and Drooling" and "You've Gotta Be Crazy."

Waters reworked some of the lyrics to fit a new concept he was working on. He was basing the new work on George Orwell's satiric novel *Animal Farm*. In the novel, farm animals represent political figures. Some animals are the rulers and some are

Barrett's Later Career

Barrett put out another solo record in November 1970, the self-titled *Barrett*. Critics felt it was better than *The Madcap Laughs* but still short of his work in Pink Floyd. His first post–Pink Floyd gig featured Gilmour on guitar, but Barrett walked offstage after four songs. Barrett formed a band called Stars in 1972, but the group disbanded after an unsuccessful concert in Cambridge. After a brief return to London—during which he showed up to his former band's *Wish You Were Here* recording session—Barrett relocated to Cambridge for good in 1978. He never recorded any more music and instead returned to his first artistic pursuit, painting. Barrett had nothing further to do with the music industry. He led a quiet life in his hometown and lived off of royalty money from his recorded music.

Gilmour's tensions with Waters's leadership grew in the years following *Wish You Were Here*.

the oppressed citizens. Waters's take was a little more focused on the politics of Britain at the time.

Waters saw a breakdown in British society caused by the policies of the country's right-wing government. "You've Gotta Be Crazy" became "Dogs." The dogs represented people who get ahead in society by preying on others. "Raving and Drooling" became "Sheep," who represented the citizenry. The other songs on the album focused on the pigs, who represented the ruling politicians. At the end of the album, the sheep rise up and kill the dogs. The album was titled *Animals*.

The rest of the band members did not disagree with Waters's political views, but they weren't as passionate as he was. The album was very much his vision. Musically, Gilmour had a lot to contribute, especially the guitar part on "Dogs." But Wright was asked to do very little. Waters was setting the course for the band, and tensions began to surface. Gilmour and Wright both felt held down by Waters, who was in full control and stifling his bandmates creatively and personally.

> "In terms of drive and lyrical concept matters, [Waters] was the de facto leader."[2]
>
> *– David Gilmour on the making of* Animals

London's Battersea Power Station was famously depicted on the *Animals* album cover.

IN THE FLESH

Even as the band's infighting grew, it hit the road to support *Animals*, which was released in January 1977. The record didn't match *Dark Side* or *Wish You Were Here* but was still a top-five album on the UK and US charts. Tickets were selling well for the subsequent In the Flesh tour across Europe and North America.

On tour, the band's visuals reached new heights. An inflatable pig watched over the stage. And in the second set, the band played *Wish You Were Here* in its entirety in front of a circular screen.

The screen showed animated films that tied into the music. The animator on these films was Gerald Scarfe, and his work became a part of Pink Floyd's visuals going forward.

Pink Floyd was playing to huge crowds around the world. But the band was worried its message was being lost in huge stadiums in front of so many people. And the tolls of touring were wearing on them and their relationships.

When Pigs Fly

Hipgnosis designed the album cover for *Animals*. It featured an inflatable pig flying over London's Battersea Power Station. The pig was 30 feet (9 m) long and was made by a German company that used to make airships.[3] On the day of the photo shoot, strong winds broke the pig free from its mooring and it flew away. It was later recovered, but there were no suitable photos to use. The pig had to be superimposed on a photo of the station to make the final album cover.

CHAPTER SEVEN

The Final Cut

The In the Flesh tour marked a turning point for Pink Floyd. The band members were disillusioned by fame and found themselves playing to huge crowds that weren't truly connecting with the music. On the last night of the tour, in Montreal, Waters noticed a group of fans toward the front of the stage causing a disturbance and not paying attention. In anger and frustration, he spat at one of the fans. That was the final straw of a stressful tour for Gilmour, who walked off stage and refused to play the encore.

The band's internal strife reached a breaking point as well. Waters began

An incident on the band's tour for *Animals* helped spawn the idea for its next album.

traveling to shows separately from the rest of the group. The tour ended in July 1977 with the band members barely speaking to one another. After that they went to work on other projects, including solo albums from Gilmour and Wright.

BUILDING A WALL

The spitting incident was upsetting for the entire band, especially Waters. Reflecting on it, he realized how distant he felt from his audience. It was like there was a wall between the band and its fans. This idea gave him inspiration for the next Pink Floyd album.

The band reconvened in the summer of 1978. Waters presented the band with two ideas. One was a concept called *Bricks in the Wall*. The other was a concept album about a man's dreams in the course of one night. Waters's bandmates all voted in favor of the wall idea. Waters already had the framework of the album in place, and he was in control from the start. The band set to work on the album that became *The Wall*.

The Wall was more of a complete narrative than Pink Floyd's previous albums. It tells the story of Pink, a famous rock star who finds himself more and more isolated from the world due to various tragedies in his life. As with Waters, Pink's father died in a war, and Pink never truly gets over that loss. Pink's persona is also based on Barrett, who was left broken by drugs and the music industry.

The rest of Pink Floyd was on board with the concept, but Waters was demanding in how it was to be executed. He was dissatisfied with the performances of all the other band members, especially Wright. Wright felt that he wasn't being given good enough material to work with. Wright decided to quit Pink Floyd after he finished his contributions to the album.

> "If somebody had a good idea, I would accept it and maybe use it. There was only one chief, and that was me."[1]
>
> – *Roger Waters on the lack of collaboration during the making of* The Wall

Waters brought in a different drummer to record the song "Mother" when he was unhappy with how Mason performed it. Gilmour struggled to get his preferred version of "Comfortably Numb" on the final album. He ended up compromising with Waters, and the song became one of *The Wall*'s most famous tracks. Later, Gilmour said that he sometimes just gave in so he wouldn't have to fight with Waters any further.

OUT OF THE STUDIO AND ON THE ROAD

Despite all the conflict, Pink Floyd completed *The Wall*, and it was released on November 30, 1979.

JOHN DENVER – SEASON OF THE HEART

PINK
FLOYD
THE
WALL

As with several other Pink Floyd albums, *The Wall*'s striking cover became famous.

It hit Number 1 in the United States, and "Another Brick in the Wall, Part 2" became the band's first Number 1 single in both the United Kingdom and United States. The album was a massive undertaking. It was more than 80 minutes in length and took up two vinyl records.

Waters had a falling out with Hipgnosis and asked Scarfe to design the album cover and interiors instead. The cover consisted of a plain, white brick wall. Inside were drawings of some of the album's characters, including a strict schoolmaster and Pink's wife. These characters were also present in the form of puppets at the live show. Nowhere to be found were the names of Wright or Mason on the album's writing credits. Wright officially left the band after the album was recorded, but he was employed as a live performer for the subsequent tour.

Another Brick

"Another Brick in the Wall, Part 2" became one of Pink Floyd's most iconic songs and famously includes vocals sung by schoolchildren. The band wanted to have the voices of actual schoolchildren in the song, which is about the mistreatment of students by teachers. The band's management contacted a local teacher who agreed to bring a group of his 13- and 14-year-old students to sing.

Waters's vision for the album included an ambitious live show. Throughout the course of performing the album, a giant wall was constructed between the band and the audience. Then at the end, when Pink overcomes his isolation, the wall came crashing down.

Because of all the work and equipment involved in producing the show, it was only held in four cities, two in the United States and two in Europe, in 1980. Waters was very satisfied with the tour and considered it the best in Pink Floyd's history. The show even spawned a feature film that was released in 1982.

The Wall: The Film

Waters's original vision for *The Wall* always included an accompanying film. At first designed as a concert film, it later morphed into a dramatic telling of *The Wall* story featuring the music as a soundtrack. Waters wanted to play the role of Pink himself but ultimately agreed to cast Irish rock musician Bob Geldof. Geldof later organized Pink Floyd's reunion at Live 8 in 2005. The film received positive reviews, especially concerning Scarfe's imagery.

TEARING DOWN THE WALL

By the end of the *Wall* tour, morale was at a low point. The band's dressing rooms, which were mobile trailers, were parked with the doors facing outward so that the band members would not have to interact with one another. In June

1981, the band played five shows in London. That was the end of Pink Floyd as a touring band.

The group planned to record a soundtrack for the film version of *The Wall* that would have extra songs that didn't make it onto the album version. That never happened. Instead, Waters proposed a new concept album, *The Final Cut*, that dealt with war and Waters's anti-war beliefs. It was specifically inspired by the British invasion of the Falkland Islands in 1982.

Pink Floyd was now a trio with the departure of Wright, and Waters exerted even more control than before. He wrote nearly everything on the new record except for Gilmour's guitar solos. Gilmour only sang on one song, "Not Now John."

Recording the follow-up to *The Wall* was difficult for the band, but *The Final Cut* still had a flair of Floydian experimentation to it. It was recorded with

The Falklands War

Roger Waters had been anti-war for his entire life, and Pink Floyd's music had explored some of those themes before. But Waters was particularly inspired to write about war on *The Final Cut*. The United Kingdom had controlled the Falkland Islands off the coast of Argentina since the 1600s. Argentina had long disagreed with this claim and tried to retake the islands in 1982. Fighting lasted 74 days, until Argentina surrendered. The conflict resulted in the deaths of more than 800 people.[2]

a technology called holophonic sound. When combined with sound effects like World War II–era airplanes whooshing past, the record's sound became almost three dimensional, as if the planes were flying above the listener.

The Final Cut was released in March 1983. Gilmour's name was eventually left off the credits entirely, and there was no tour planned. It still went to Number 6 in the United States and Number 1 in the United Kingdom, where it actually outperformed *The Wall*.

AN UNCERTAIN FUTURE

Gilmour's and Waters's next steps reflected their personal ambitions for their future careers. Gilmour recorded a new solo album and then went on tour. The tour had nothing resembling a Pink Floyd show's usual impressive visuals and theatrics. Instead it focused more on the music and Gilmour's guitar. Gilmour enjoyed the freedom to do something different from Pink Floyd. He took the tour into smaller venues and avoided stadiums. But he still planned to return to Pink Floyd someday.

Waters recorded his solo album a month before the release of *The Final Cut*. It was called *The Pros and Cons of Hitchhiking*. The album was based on the other concept Waters had presented to Pink Floyd before they settled on *The Wall*. Waters

Waters went on a short US tour for *The Pros and Cons of Hitchhiking* in 1984.

had big-name musicians contribute to the record, including guitar icon Eric Clapton, who also played on Waters's tour.

Unlike Gilmour, who chose to play small venues, Waters's solo tour hit large arenas. He performed in front of animations designed by Scarfe. Waters also included Pink Floyd material on the set list. Overall, the tour was not a financial success. There was not as much interest in the members of Pink Floyd individually as there was for the band itself.

CHAPTER EIGHT

Coming Back to Life

The night before Gilmour's last London show of his 1984 tour, he approached Mason and Wright with an idea. He asked whether they would be willing to play on "Comfortably Numb" during that final show. It had been years since they'd played together, but the pair agreed and enjoyed performing. This was the closest thing to a Pink Floyd reunion during this time.

Gilmour, Mason, and Wright continued to meet occasionally. Gilmour and Mason thought this period was just another hiatus in Pink Floyd's history. But that was not Waters's understanding. Throughout 1985, Waters insisted that he would not be returning to

From left, Gilmour, Mason, and Wright continued Pink Floyd without Waters in the mid-1980s.

Pink Floyd. Not only that but he wished that the band would dissolve so he could pursue a solo career without a band called Pink Floyd continuing to tour and play his songs. Gilmour and Mason were undecided and thought they might want to continue the band.

Waters finally tried to force the band out of business in December 1985. He wrote to EMI to declare that Pink Floyd was a "spent force creatively" and that the band ceased to exist.[1] But Waters did not have the final say on that matter.

LEGAL BATTLES

A war of words and lawyers began between Waters on one side and Gilmour and Mason on the other. Waters insisted that nobody had the right to use the name Pink Floyd without him. Gilmour and Mason were convinced that Waters was just trying to scare them into going away.

In early 1986, Gilmour and Mason decided they were going to continue Pink Floyd and started putting together plans to record a new Pink Floyd album. They recruited new musicians and one old one. Once Wright heard that Waters had left the band, he was willing to return.

Waters was enraged. He filed a lawsuit trying to force the band to dissolve. He even publicly released his letter to EMI. The others put out a statement of their own. It said that while they wished Waters well, he was no longer in the band and the three of them were making a new album.

FLOATING ON

The threat of a lawsuit dangled over their heads, but Gilmour, Mason, and Wright pressed on. Rehearsals started on Gilmour's houseboat on the River Thames in England. Waters continued to put out public statements seeking to disband Pink Floyd. But legally, the record label found that no one person owned the rights to the name.

The trio of Pink Floyd released *A Momentary Lapse of Reason* in September 1987. Mason and Wright performed on the record, but it was mostly Gilmour's creation. Nonetheless, there was still public appetite for Pink Floyd's music. The album hit Number 3 in both the United Kingdom and

Visiting Venice

As part of the *Momentary Lapse of Reason* tour, Pink Floyd agreed to play a free show in Venice, Italy. In the city of canals there was no place to set up a stage, so the band instead played on a floating stage in a lagoon. It was a beautiful scene, but concert organizers failed to plan properly for the crowd. Approximately 200,000 people showed up to catch a glimpse of the band.[2] The town was overrun with people and the garbage they produced. It was such a failure for the city that Venice's city council resigned in disgrace.

Pink Floyd put on a massive outdoor concert in Berlin, Germany, in 1988.

United States. Waters dismissed it as "a pretty fair forgery."[3]

One thing that was just like the old Pink Floyd was the album cover. For the first time since *Animals*, Thorgerson and Hipgnosis designed a Pink Floyd cover. The cover photograph depicted

800 hospital beds across the shores of Devon in the southwest of England.

Pink Floyd had managed to make a record, but touring was different. The trio had not played a full show together since 1981. There was no guarantee that fans would be waiting for them. Few corporate sponsors were willing to fund the tour, and Gilmour and Mason had to offer up $3 million by themselves.[4]

The first show sold out as soon as tickets went on sale. Then the second did, too. The North American leg of the *Momentary Lapse of Reason* tour lasted three months. It featured most of the same Pink Floyd visuals that fans loved. Gilmour, Mason, and Wright were enjoying playing together again for enthusiastic crowds.

A TRUCE

Meanwhile, Waters was touring his next solo record, *Radio K.A.O.S.* Unlike his former bandmates, he was struggling to attract fans. Nobody was minimizing Waters's contributions to Pink Floyd. But fans seemed more excited to go see a band performing as Pink Floyd rather than Waters performing Pink Floyd songs.

The former bandmates finally agreed to a settlement in late 1987. Waters conceded that Gilmour, Mason, and Wright could perform as Pink Floyd. But they agreed to give up rights to certain Waters creations, such as the concept of *The Wall* and the inflatable pig. That matter was settled, but the two parties were still angry with each other.

Pink Floyd concluded the North American portion of its tour in 1988. The final show was recorded for a live album called *A Delicate Sound of Thunder* that was released in November of that year. It reached Number 11 in both the United States and United Kingdom. The tour continued throughout Europe into the summer of 1989.

NO MORE DIVISION

Waters showed he could still put on a major stage production in 1990. Always conscious of world events, he staged a concert on the former site of the Berlin Wall. The Berlin Wall was built to separate East and West Germany following World War II. Its demolition in 1989 reunited Germany into one country. Waters performed *The Wall* on the site and donated the proceeds to charity. The production sold 180,000 tickets, but the crowd was estimated at up to 300,000 people.[5] Waters released a film of the concert and then recorded his third solo album, *Amused to Death*, in 1992. The album did not sell well enough to merit a tour.

A Near-Death Experience

In a break after the *Momentary Lapse of Reason* tour, Mason, Gilmour, and band manager Steve O'Rourke raced in the Carrera Panamericana auto race in Mexico. They planned to make a film and then provide a soundtrack for it. Gilmour and O'Rourke were in a car together, and they crashed. The vehicle left the road at 80 miles per hour (130 kmh), but amazingly Gilmour was unhurt and O'Rourke only suffered a broken leg.[6]

Waters's 1990 performance of *The Wall* took on additional significance when performed at the site of the infamous Berlin Wall.

By January 1993, Pink Floyd was ready to return to the studio. Unlike in 1986, when Mason and Wright were out of practice and the group was relearning how to play together, the members felt more like a well-functioning band. They often jammed together to come up with new ideas, just like in the early days of the band.

The result of these sessions was 1994's *The Division Bell*. Similar in sound to *Momentary Lapse*, it highlighted Gilmour's guitar and vocals. The album cover was again designed by Hipgnosis. It showed two giant metal heads facing each other in conversation. The importance of communication was a major theme of the lyrics.

STILL A PULSE

Pink Floyd hit the road for another world tour in March 1994. A giant circular screen was designed for the stage. It displayed visuals, rotated, and shined

A Special Guest Vocalist

Communication was a major theme of *The Division Bell*. With this in mind, the band featured a guest vocalist who was an expert on the subject. But he wasn't a singer. Physicist Stephen Hawking lent his voice to the song "Keep Talking." The words were about how important it is for humanity to keep talking to one another to solve problems. However, Hawking didn't record the words specifically for the album. The clip came from a telephone commercial.

lights down on the band. The set also included a powerful laser show. It involved two lasers, each costing $120,000, that were designed for high-speed photography and nuclear research.[7] The lasers were so bright they required Federal Aviation Administration permission when used outdoors.

> "We're all playing and functioning much better than we were after the trials and tribulations of the late Roger years."[8]
>
> *– David Gilmour, interview with* Guitar World *magazine, 1987*

The Division Bell went to Number 1 in the United Kingdom and the United States. As the tour stretched into 1995, the band began playing *The Dark Side of the Moon* in its entirety at every show. These shows were captured on the live film and album *Pulse*.

Pink Floyd concluded the tour with a 14-night run at Earls Court in London. The tour was a massive success. It earned more in six

Publius Enigma

Shortly after the *Division Bell* tour began, a mysterious person began posting online on the Pink Floyd message boards. Going only by the name Publius, he or she left a series of clues indicating there was a puzzle to be solved within the album. Publius also predicted there would be a message during a Pink Floyd concert in New Jersey. And that night, the words *PUBLIUS* and *ENIGMA* appeared on stage. The band later said the puzzle was a marketing ploy by its record label. The puzzle has not yet been solved.

months than the *Momentary Lapse* tour had earned in two and a half years.[9] But after the final note rang out in Earls Court, it was unclear whether the band would ever play together again.

CHAPTER NINE

The Song Is Over

The next time the world saw Pink Floyd, it was in 1996 at the Rock & Roll Hall of Fame. The band was receiving its induction. Only Gilmour, Mason, and Wright attended. Waters and Barrett were invited but declined. Gilmour and Wright performed a version of "Wish You Were Here" at the ceremony.

But after that, the Pink Floyd world went dark. The band reported no plans for a new album or tour. Waters, who had largely not worked since his 1992 solo album, began touring again in 1999. He played his solo music as well as Pink Floyd music from his time in the band. Waters toured extensively

The Rock & Roll Hall of Fame is located in Cleveland, Ohio.

ELVIS IS IN THE BUILDING
ROCK AND ROLL HALL OF FAME AN
ONE

throughout the early 2000s. He was in fact the only member of Pink Floyd touring in 2005. The sudden announcement that Pink Floyd would reunite at Live 8 took everyone by surprise. That special night in London was one of the band's most memorable performances. But it would also be their last.

Rock Hall

Pieces of Pink Floyd history have gone into the Rock & Roll Hall of Fame. Two giant items from the first *The Wall* tour are prominently displayed in the museum. The exhibit includes a section of the actual wall set that was assembled and then destroyed during the show and a 20-foot- (6 m) long puppet that depicted the teacher character from the album.[2]

ON SEPARATE ISLANDS

Gilmour released his solo album *On an Island* in 2006. It was his most successful solo album and sparked a world tour. Wright was with him in the touring band. Waters launched a marathon tour of *The Dark Side of the Moon* in 2006 that eventually included 110 concerts.[1] Waters performed the album in its entirety in the second half of the show. Both Waters and Gilmour continued to deny any rumors of a reunion.

Tragedy brought the band together again. Barrett died in July 2006 at the age of 60. None of the band attended his funeral, wanting to give his family privacy and not draw more publicity. But all four band members were in attendance at a tribute concert in May 2007. Gilmour, Mason, and Wright performed "Arnold Layne." Waters performed one of his solo songs.

Any hope of all four members playing together again was lost in September 2008. Wright died of cancer at the age of 65. His work on keyboards helped create the band's atmospheric music, something Wright's former bandmates pointed out in the aftermath of his loss.

> "Pink Floyd are the ultimate rock and roll anomaly. They sold massive amounts of records, have always been a popular live band, and they were never a singles driven band, a lesson forever needed to be learned in this particular business. Because they've always stood for, been about, music. And why? Because it is the people who listen to music that drives the business, not the other way around."[3]
>
> *– Smashing Pumpkins front man Billy Corgan inducting Pink Floyd into the Rock & Roll Hall of Fame, 1996*

BACK ATOP THE WALL

In 2010, Waters mounted another version of a *Wall* tour. It was still the same music from the album, but the show wasn't anything like how it had been done before. Waters's new wall was massive and used

Gilmour continued touring into the 2000s and 2010s.

15 high-definition projectors to cast images on the wall. The show used the same Scarfe imagery but updated it with computer animation. The wall could move and sway back and forth. But the high point of the show was the same: the wall came crashing down all at once.

Waters also updated the message of the show. Instead of being about Pink's isolation, it was a metaphor for how societies and nations isolate themselves. "Fear Builds Walls" was a slogan used in the show, and Waters encouraged the destruction of walls, real and imagined.[4] The show was a huge success and set a record for highest-grossing tour by a solo artist at the time.

Gilmour's Guitars

Gilmour assembled a remarkable collection of guitars throughout his career in Pink Floyd. In 2019, he decided to thin his collection while also raising money for a good cause. Gilmour put more than 120 guitars out of his collection up for auction. Proceeds of the sale went to ClientEarth, which helps fight climate change. The most expensive guitar was his 1969 black Fender Stratocaster. The "Black Strat" was used on nearly every Pink Floyd album from 1970 to 1983. It sold for a record $3,975,000.[5]

The rebooted *Wall* tour ran through 2013, but the highlight for fans came in 2011. Waters had previously appeared at a charity concert as a favor to Gilmour. In thanks, Gilmour promised he would perform "Comfortably Numb" at one of Waters's

Waters's *Wall* shows continued to be dramatic, large-scale productions.

Wall shows. That day came on May 12, 2011. It was a total surprise to fans in attendance. To make the surprise even better, Mason joined Waters and Gilmour on tambourine for "Outside the Wall," the last song on the album and last song of the show. It was the first time those three members had performed together since Live 8. And it was the last time.

"Thirty years ago when David and Nick and I first did this, I was a rather grumpy person, disaffected with rock and roll audiences as young David will attest. But all that's changed—I could not be happier than to be in this room with these two guys and all of you here tonight."[6]

– Roger Waters alongside Gilmour and Mason in 2011

THE ENDLESS RIVER

But there was good news and new material on the horizon for Pink Floyd fans. Gilmour and Mason started reviewing tapes from the *Division Bell* recording sessions. There was quite a lot of material to work with, and a lot of it featured Wright. Releasing it would serve as a kind of tribute to their friend.

This music became 2014's *The Endless River*. The album was all instrumentals except for one track, which was by Gilmour and his wife, Polly Sampson. Thorgerson had died the year before, but his Hipgnosis collaborator Aubrey

Powell designed the cover. It depicted a young man propelling a boat over a sea of clouds.

After its release, Gilmour confirmed there would be no tour, and he said the album was the band's last. But the album showed that the band was still incredibly popular. It was the most preordered album ever on Amazon.com and the fastest-selling vinyl record in 17 years.[7] The band was still beloved, even 50 years after its debut.

Nick Mason's Saucerful of Secrets

A relatively unexplored part of the Pink Floyd catalog has been the band's early career with Syd Barrett. Most tours by Pink Floyd, as well as by the band's individual members working as solo acts, focused on *The Dark Side of the Moon* and later. But Mason set out to change that in 2019. He and some longtime Floyd collaborators launched Nick Mason's Saucerful of Secrets tour. The set list consisted of music from 1971 and earlier. Waters joined the band to play "A Saucerful of Secrets" at a show in New York City in April of that year.

LOOKING BACK

Pink Floyd left behind an impressive legacy. The band's early melding of R&B with psychedelic rock created a new kind of art rock that was an influence for many musicians and bands, including David Bowie, Queen, and Radiohead. Their sound effects and ambient music created a unique sound. And they mixed it all with an impressive live visual display that dazzled audiences. Even the artwork on their album covers, especially for *The Dark Side of the Moon* and *The Wall*, remains iconic in rock history.

Pink Floyd's members all had successful careers on their own, but nothing was quite the same as what they did together. Barrett's, and later Waters's, creativity, Gilmour's guitar, Mason's steady timekeeping, and Wright's atmospheric keyboards were all crucial to the Pink Floyd sound.

Though the band's core lineup split up sooner than fans would have liked, Pink Floyd made a profound impression on the evolution of rock and roll. They sold 250 million records and are widely considered one of the greatest bands of all time.[8] It hardly matters that their greatest hits came out decades ago. Their classic music continues to find new audiences. The special Pink Floyd sound is just a play button away.

TIMELINE

1966
Pink Floyd plays their first show under that name with their original quartet: Syd Barrett, Roger Waters, Nick Mason, and Richard Wright.

1967
The band records its first single, "Arnold Layne," in January; its first full-length album, *The Piper at the Gates of Dawn*, is released in August.

1968
Pink Floyd announces the departure of founding member Barrett. He is replaced by guitarist David Gilmour. *A Saucerful of Secrets* is released.

1973
The band releases *The Dark Side of the Moon* in March, which hits Number 1 in the United States.

1975
Barrett shows up at a recording session for *Wish You Were Here*. It is the last time the whole band sees him.

1977
Pink Floyd releases *Animals* in January.

1979
Wright officially quits the band after conflicts with Waters; *The Wall* is released in November.

1980

The band embarks on the ambitious *Wall* tour. Wright performs with the group as a paid musician.

1983

Pink Floyd releases *The Final Cut*, its last record with Waters.

1985

Waters quits the band, later declaring it a "spent force creatively."

1987

A reformed Pink Floyd with Gilmour, Mason, and Wright releases *A Momentary Lapse of Reason*.

1994

Pink Floyd releases *The Division Bell*.

2005

Waters, Gilmour, Mason, and Wright reunite to perform at the Live 8 charity concert.

2006

Syd Barrett dies at age 60.

2008

Richard Wright dies of cancer at age 65.

2014

Gilmour and Mason pull together recordings from the *Division Bell* sessions to release one final Pink Floyd album, *The Endless River*.

ESSENTIAL FACTS

Pink Floyd Band Members

- **Syd Barrett** was Pink Floyd's original singer and songwriter. He left the group in 1968.
- **Richard Wright** played keyboards in Pink Floyd.
- **Roger Waters** played bass and became Pink Floyd's primary creative force following Barrett's departure.
- **Nick Mason** played the drums in Pink Floyd.
- **David Gilmour** played guitar, creating many of the band's iconic solos.

Pink Floyd Studio Albums

- *The Piper at the Gates of Dawn* (1967)
- *A Saucerful of Secrets* (1968)
- *More* (1969)
- *Ummagumma* (1969)
- *Atom Heart Mother* (1970)
- *Meddle* (1971)
- *Obscured by Clouds* (1972)
- *The Dark Side of the Moon* (1973)
- *Wish You Were Here* (1975)
- *Animals* (1977)
- *The Wall* (1979)
- *The Final Cut* (1983)
- *A Momentary Lapse of Reason* (1987)
- *The Division Bell* (1994)
- *The Endless River* (2014)

Career Highlights

Pink Floyd is one of the most commercially successful bands of all time and one of just eight bands in history to sell 250 million records or more. The group had seven albums that hit Number 1 in either the United Kingdom or United States or both: *Atom Heart Mother, The Dark Side of the Moon, Wish You Were Here, The Wall, The Final Cut, The Division Bell*, and *The Endless River.* The band was inducted into the Rock & Roll Hall of Fame in 1996.

Conflicts

Two of Pink Floyd's founding members left the band under difficult circumstances. Guitarist, vocalist, and primary songwriter Barrett was removed from the band in 1968 due to his drug use and erratic behavior. He was replaced by Gilmour. Bassist and principal songwriter Waters left the band in 1985, later suing his former bandmates, who continued to perform as Pink Floyd.

Quote

"[Our way of working was] finding something we can do individually that other people haven't tried, like provoking the most extraordinary sounds from a piano by scratching around inside it."

—Nick Mason, Pink Floyd: Behind the Wall, *2013*

GLOSSARY

bass line
The part of a song played on the bass guitar.

bill
A list of performers in a concert.

chord
A combination of notes played at the same time.

concept album
An album that is organized around a single theme or story.

conscientious objector
Someone who chooses not to participate in military service based on their beliefs about war.

debut
The first appearance, often of an album or publication, made by a musician or group.

discography
A complete list of a band's recordings.

gig
A job for a musician, actor, or other performer.

hallucinogenic
Causing hallucinations, or things that are sensed but aren't actually there.

instrumental
A song that has no words.

jamming
Playing music casually with no set end.

leg
A segment of a concert tour usually covering one geographic area.

lyrics
The words to a song.

psychedelic
Influenced by the drug culture of hallucinations and altered perceptions.

record label
A company that promotes and publishes a band's music.

repertoire
The body of music a performer is capable of playing.

R&B
Rhythm and blues; a type of pop music of African American origin that has a soulful vocal style that features improvisation.

set list
The list of songs a band plays during a concert.

single
A song or track released to the public independently, not as part of a complete album.

synthesizer
An electronic musical instrument, usually with a keyboard, that can make a wide variety of sounds by combining signals of different frequencies.

time signature
The notation of how many beats are in a measure of music.

ADDITIONAL RESOURCES

Selected Bibliography

Blake, Mark. *Comfortably Numb: The Inside Story of Pink Floyd*. Thunder's Mouth Press, 2008.

Fielder, Hugh. *Pink Floyd: Behind the Wall*. Race Point, 2013.

Mason, Nick. *Inside Out: A Personal History of Pink Floyd*. Chronicle Books, 2017.

Further Readings

Cummings, Judy Dodge. *The Beatles*. Abdo, 2022.

Guilleminot, Hervé. *40 Inspiring Icons: Music Legends*. Wide-Eyed, 2018.

Moore, Shannon Baker. *A History of Music*. Abdo, 2015.

To learn more about Pink Floyd, please visit **abdobooklinks.com** or scan this QR code. These links are routinely monitored and updated to provide the most current information available.

More Information

For more information on this subject, contact or visit the following organizations:

Pink Floyd: Their Mortal Remains
pinkfloydexhibition.es/en/

This traveling Pink Floyd exhibition features a collection of artifacts from the band's 50-year history. Started in London in 2017, the exhibition is scheduled to tour internationally for ten years.

Rock & Roll Hall of Fame
1100 Rock and Roll Blvd.
Cleveland, OH 44114
216-781-7625
rockhall.com

Pink Floyd was inducted into the Rock & Roll Hall of Fame in 1996. Fans can see artifacts from the band's career and learn about its history.

SOURCE NOTES

CHAPTER 1. BACK IN LONDON

1. "Pink Floyd Live at Live 8 London." *YouTube*, uploaded by Michele Matraia, 8 Dec. 2014, youtube.com/watch?v=ljaU7YcrKAU. Accessed 21 Jan. 2020.

2. "'Live Aid' Concert Raises $127 Million for Famine Relief in Africa." *History*, n.d., history.com. Accessed 10 Feb. 2020.

3. Robert Sandall. "Pink Floyd Reunion Proves that Pigs Can Fly." *Telegraph*, 30 June 2005, telegraph.co.uk. Accessed 21 Jan. 2020.

4. "Pink Floyd Live at Live 8 London."

5. "Pink Floyd Live at Live 8 London."

6. "Pink Floyd Live at Live 8 London."

7. Austin Scaggs. "Q&A: Roger Waters." *Rolling Stone*, 11 Aug. 2005, rollingstone.com. Accessed 21 Jan. 2020.

8. Nick Deriso. "Revisiting Pink Floyd's Reunion at Live 8." *Ultimate Classic Rock*, 2 July 2015, ultimateclassicrock.com. Accessed 21 Jan. 2020.

9. Deriso, "Revisiting Pink Floyd's Reunion at Live 8."

CHAPTER 2. FRIENDS AND BANDMATES

1. Mark Blake. *Comfortably Numb: The Inside Story of Pink Floyd.* Da Capo Press, 2008. 12.

2. Hugh Fielder. *Pink Floyd: Behind the Wall*. Race Point Publishing, 2013. 19.

CHAPTER 3. AT THE GATES OF DAWN

1. Hugh Fielder. *Pink Floyd: Behind the Wall*. Race Point Publishing, 2013. 22.

2. Nick Mason. *Inside Out: A Personal History of Pink Floyd*. Chronicle Books, 2017. 107–108.

3. Fielder, *Pink Floyd: Behind the Wall*, 31.

CHAPTER 4. MOVING ON AND CHANGING SIDES

1. Hugh Fielder. *Pink Floyd: Behind the Wall*. Race Point Publishing, 2013. 42.

2. Fielder, *Pink Floyd: Behind the Wall*, 44.

CHAPTER 5. THE DAM BREAKS OPEN

1. "David Gilmour." *Rolling Stone*, 12 Mar. 2003, lawos.heimat.eu. Accessed 21 Jan. 2020.

2. Luca Divelti. "The Great Gig in the Sky: the Story of Pink Floyd's Gem." *Aural Crave*, 27 May 2018, auralcrave.com. Accessed 21 Jan. 2020.

3. Hugh Fielder. *Pink Floyd: Behind the Wall*. Race Point Publishing, 2013. 90.

4. Nick Mason. *Inside Out: A Personal History of Pink Floyd*. Chronicle Books, 2017. 187.

CHAPTER 6. THE SAME OLD FEARS

1. "Pink Floyd- Wish You Were Here- Roger Waters, David Gilmour, Nick Mason." *In the Studio with Redbeard*, 2020, inthestudio.net. Accessed 21 Jan. 2020.

2. Hugh Fielder. *Pink Floyd: Behind the Wall*. Race Point Publishing, 2013. 116.

3. Nick Mason. *Inside Out: A Personal History of Pink Floyd*. Chronicle Books, 2017. 325–327.

SOURCE NOTES CONTINUED

CHAPTER 7. THE FINAL CUT

1. Hugh Fielder. *Pink Floyd: Behind the Wall*. Race Point Publishing, 2013. 133.
2. Fielder, *Pink Floyd: Behind the Wall*, 156.

CHAPTER 8. COMING BACK TO LIFE

1. Hugh Fielder. *Pink Floyd: Behind the Wall*. Race Point Publishing, 2013. 163.
2. Fielder, *Pink Floyd: Behind the Wall*,180.
3. Fielder, *Pink Floyd: Behind the Wall*, 169.
4. Fielder, *Pink Floyd: Behind the Wall*,169.
5. Fielder, *Pink Floyd: Behind the Wall*, 181.
6. Nick Mason. *Inside Out: A Personal History of Pink Floyd*. Chronicle Books, 2017. 482–484.
7. Catherine McHugh. "Welcome to the Machine." *Lighting Dimensions*, Sept. 1994, pink-floyd.org. Accessed 21 Jan. 2020.
8. Fielder, *Pink Floyd: Behind the Wall*, 187.
9. Fielder, *Pink Floyd: Behind the Wall*, 187–190.

CHAPTER 9. THE SONG IS OVER

1. Hugh Fielder. *Pink Floyd: Behind the Wall.* Race Point Publishing, 2013. 200–201.

2. Troy L. Smith. "Rock Hall Preps for the Return of Pink Floyd's 'The Wall' & Teacher." *Cleveland.com*, 11 Jan. 2019, cleveland.com. Accessed 21 Jan. 2020.

3. Billy Corgan. "1996 Rock'N'Roll Hall of Fame: Pink Floyd Induction Speech." *Brain Damage*, 17 Jan. 1996, brain-damage.co.uk. Accessed 21 Jan. 2020.

4. Fielder, *Pink Floyd: Behind the Wall*, 204–206.

5. Kory Grow. "David Gilmour's Guitars Sell for Millions at Charity Auction." *Rolling Stone*, 20 June 2019, rollingstone.com. Accessed 21 Jan. 2020.

6. Fielder, *Pink Floyd: Behind the Wall*, 208.

7. Nick Mason. *Inside Out: A Personal History of Pink Floyd*. Chronicle Books, 2017. 543.

8. "Pink Floyd." *Rock & Roll Hall of Fame*, n.d., rockhall.com. Accessed 21 Jan. 2020.

INDEX

ABOUT THE AUTHOR

Todd Kortemeier

Todd Kortemeier wasn't even born when Roger Waters was a member of Pink Floyd, but thanks to his dad's vinyl collection, he grew up listening to and loving the band. He lives near Minneapolis with his wife, their daughter, and their dachshund/beagle mix.